Crossing the Bridge

. . . .

A discussion between a father and his son on how to connect with

the new work force.

Special Thanks To:

Alissa

Eileen

John

Kathy

Mike

Rebecca

Rick

Introduction

I want to thank you for reading this work on how to build a relationship with and manage the new workforce being pumped out of today's colleges. If you bought the book- great for us; we appreciate your support. If you downloaded and printed a copy, welcome to the new world of publishing.

This is the first collaborative writing project for my son and me. We are excited about the project and about the opportunity to help calm the nerves of the workforce. We hope to shed some light on a difficult issue. I am a Human Resource professional and have worked in manufacturing for my whole career. I graduated from Western Illinois University in the mid 70's and studied fine arts.

My son graduated from Columbia College in Chicago in 2009 and is working as a customer service supervisor for an online company that sells products to the music industry. He is a writer, producer and performer so his job fits him well.

We have had several discussions on supervising and management which has led us to start taking notes and putting this book together. Our goal is to share our ideas and thoughts on what has been successful and what has failed to help the reader get a better grasp on managing the new workforce.

I am a 24-year-old Lead Supervisor at a call center in downtown Chicago. I have been a manager or supervisor at every job I have held, save a couple in the beginning. I assume that most people have downloaded this or had it emailed from a friend. My only question is who did it? Who took the time to digitalize a copy? I'm not going to lie; I am flattered at how long that must have taken.

The idea behind this book is what my Dad just said; help bridge the gap between managers and the new workforce. We all have to work together so lets do it as painlessly and productively as possible. Have fun and good luck.

Table of contents

Who are these people?

"A man who is not a Liberal at sixteen has no heart; a man who is not a Conservative at sixty has no head." ~Benjamin Disraeli

These are people who graduated college in the past five or so years and who will be coming out of colleges for some time to come. They are coming from the junior colleges, technical schools and universities. They are skilled, they are talented, and they look different. When was the last time any of them wore a tie or dress? They have taken casual Friday to a completely new level.

Some were raised in split homes, they are getting married later in life, and they have a short attention span. Most things have been provided to them early in their lives. When they were growing up they saw parents who had good jobs and fun toys, and just expected the same. Most of these new employees are skilled in at least one gaming counsel and are familiar with several social networks.

They are worried about their future and are as well-informed as anyone in the news of the world. They distrust government leadership and I find myself in agreement. They have heard stories from their parents about protesting and changing the world with new ideas but they don't seem to be able to gather the steam or develop a following to get what they think they want.

They don't necessarily see the company as their future. You have them as long as you keep them entertained. Their attention span is short on day to day activities and short on their career plans.

Remember the saying to not trust anyone over 30? The concept is

still around.

We are a generation of computers, video games and phones that can almost drive your car. What technology excels in is change; it constantly introduces new ideas, which are often a step towards a positive evolution. This means that we are used to new concepts and new protocol, so when earth-shattering ideas come around, we take them in stride. I can remember when Google came out, but I know that my younger sister, who was four years old at the time, cannot. It was integrated into my work flow on a computer so smoothly that I did not notice. We expect quick answers and instant gratification.

Video games have short answers that are very straight forward. You either completed the level or you failed. I like to know quickly whether or not my answers are correct, and cannot understand why it would take a long time for feedback. More than receiving feedback, we all want the opportunity to give our own opinions and ideas, and to speak our minds about *how we feel.*

Worrying about the best way to word negative feedback or disciplinary action is a thing of the past. When I have to tell an employee that something is wrong I know what they expect:

"Steve you told a customer that you were not sure if that software was compatible with their operating system. Did you download the manual and check?" I ask after I pull the employee into a conference room.

"Yea I checked it out but couldn't find it. I don't know... it doesn't really say" Steve answers confidently.

"OK well it's on the last page in the specifications and requirements for the software. Let me show you where to find it. In the future you need to check the spec's every time." I tell him calmly and matter-of-factly as I am demonstrating where to locate the information.

"Alright sorry, I'll do that next time." He says sounding fairly sincere.

Tell me what I did wrong, how I could have done it better, and let's move on. We do not need to be told the same thing five different ways in one meeting. We listen, decide how we are going to react then act. After you understand exactly what we expect you will most likely find that we will be some of the best employees you have.

Authority will be followed and tolerated if we respect the people who are in charge. If I do not think that my boss is right, there is a very good chance that I am not going to follow his or her directions. Even though I know that it may cost me my job, I am not going to take unnecessary or misunderstood steps to get to the same goal. Even during this recession, we have the belief that jobs are everywhere. We act like we do not need the job when we often do. Bills and responsibilities do not have an age restriction and they affect certain people in different ways. There might be no chance of me actually having enough money to pay all of my bills this month, but do you know what I am going to do on Friday night? Yes, you guessed it; I am going out and not worrying about my tab until I sign the receipt. If I am already going to be short what is another $60? There are two clear words for this with the older generation: responsibility and maturity or I guess the lack thereof.

The line "live everyday like it is your last" is an internal subconscious *mantra for the younger workers and it is reflected through actions in the workplace. It also is the idea on which our world revolves so if you catch someone from the younger generation in a casual conversation, expect comments of short sightedness and an overall lack of long term repercussion.*

Who are we?

"Each generation wants new symbols, new people, new names. They want to divorce themselves from their predecessors". ~Jim Morrison

We come from a time when parents wanted better for us and they worked to show us the way. Growing up in the "change the world" sixties, the apathy of the seventies, and the disco of the eighties made us who we are. We did what our parents wanted and found success. We bought when we wanted and lived a good life. Our focus is on ourselves; the organization always came in second. The products made in the seventies and eighties all had planned obsolesce. Cars were made to last 70,000 miles and no one seemed to care. We would just buy a new one. People did very well and some got very rich. The stock market of the 90's was incredible. Everyone was getting along just fine. All you had to do was contribute to your 401k plan and your investments did well.

To our children, we showed that everyone could get lucky once in a while. The fire of the sixties had gone out and we just wanted everyone to get along. We started to protect our children at all cost and from everything. We taught them to play the game and everyone is a winner. Everyone got a trophy at the end of the season. Do the words, "There is only one winner and everyone else is a loser" ring any bells? We remember Super bowl winners but cannot remember who they played.

Up until a few years ago we had the authority to have it done our way. Now we look around the organization and say, "Who are these people?" They demand equality and think it is owed to them. They don't seem to have the same focus we have.

We learned management techniques from a good supervisor, reading books and experimenting, or we just figured it out ourselves by treating people the way we wanted to be treated. Some worked, some did not. If you had the opportunity to work for one of the Fortune companies you may have had some formalized management/supervisory training to coincide with a career plan or recent promotion. Working in the small- and medium-sized companies, this type of training is called on-the-job-training.

We made it to a management position with some skill but we

are still learning. Events happen today with no precedent and we manage by our gut. We have done a lot of good but this is a new group of people and many of the rules have changed. Performance appraisals just do not work. The annual ritual has run it course and something different has to be done.

You look out side your office and you see this youngster with hair that will not move in a wind storm wearing cloths that seem two sizes too big and you hesitate. This person is talented and a value to the company yet you just don't see or feel any connection. This employee has a couple of tattoos and three boxes hanging from their belt. A problem comes up; as manager you need this person's help and he quickly solves the problem. You are satisfied and the employee feels accomplished. You reach to shake their hand to say thank you and you have no idea what is going to happen. Will you have to touch elbows or do the handshake dance? You just don't know. This employee is gracious and shakes hands and says thank you. You are pleasantly surprised and feel a little more comfortable.

Now this employee has saved the day and you may feel a slight connection but would you have them over for dinner?

You are the people that have given us life and hopefully did the best you could do with your resources. You are the age, or close to the age, of everyone that has ever told us to do something. From teachers to parents to police to bosses it is not typically (or not possibly) kids our age who hold these positions. What that means is that you have an ingrained authority that we may or may not like. First impressions are very important but can quickly be over looked. I expect bosses to exert an air of authority but also do not need to be suffocating.

I know you are in charge; get over it. My generation has mouths like sailors and minds driven by imagination. You probably do not want to know what we are thinking. Eventually we will have something funny to say, and may start a long conversation about things that have nothing to do with work, but we have friends and do not plan to call our boss one of them. That being said, respect is a highly valued factor so a boss showing interest in their employee outside of work, will not be seen negatively.

What does not work?

"Each generation imagines itself to be more intelligent than the one that went before it, and wiser than the one that comes after it." ~George Orwell

How is your communication program in the office? Not only is there a generation difference there is a social and technology difference. These future managers are demanding and they want things a current manager would never think of asking for. There is arrogance about them and they want rewards without putting in the time. The thought of doing the annual performance appraisal with this group keeps a manager up at night. New techniques and new ideas are needed to manage this new group.

Will using the tried and true MBO, management by objectives, work with this new generation? A manager may like this approach because they are comfortable with it, but this new group of workers needs some real-time recognition and there in lies a disconnect.

There are a lot of different ways to manage people. A lot of books have been written about what you can do and what methods have worked in the past. The reality is that no one technique or protocol is going to be effective for every work force. What works for my office is not going to be the same thing that works for yours. One of the biggest and sometimes most difficult jobs for a manager is understanding what works and what does not.

While this is something that people discuss and conceptualize ideas about, it can be one of the easiest things to find out. Ask for feedback from the people you are in charge of. I will let you know if something is not working out. In fact, I will probably not wait for you to ask and will tell you when it is not working out and bring it to your attention.

What works?

"Few will have the greatness to bend history itself; but each of us can work to change a small portion of events, and in the total; of all those acts will be written the history of this generation."

~Robert Kennedy

Over the years human nature has not changed. We all have wants and needs; we just need some help figuring out the difference. In the workplace these new employees want to be recognized and rewarded just like anyone else. However, today there are new issues and different career paths. We need to set up a system where these new employees feel they contribute, and one which gives them the freedom to make positive choices for the company.

In the past, if an employee needed a new computer you would probably have the IT department or office manager place an order and the employee would get what ever that person purchases. Why not just let the new employee purchase the computer and tell them to get what ever software they are comfortable with. If you hired them you should trust they will make a sensible decision.

We finally hit the word *trust*. You knew it was going to be in this book somewhere. Some keys to establishing good working relationships are trust, freedom, and allowing accountability for their part of the business. Micro managers are out. Occasionally verify and redirect, of course, but let them grow naturally and at their pace.

We all have fears and fear is a good thing. What does the new employee fear? Being fired, loss of self esteem, not being accepted as part of the success of the business. The key here is to reach out on an informal basis and pump them up. Tell them about the whole project and not just their part. You might be surprised what you learn from them.

What works with us is being direct and providing consistent feedback. While it may seem like it is going to be more work, what you end up with is someone who understands exactly what is expected of them. When I give feedback to an employee, there is no sugar-coating and no beating around the bush. "That was wrong, you should have done this" is about as in-depth as it gets. People know when they do something wrong, that much is not lost in the younger crowds, but what is lost is the sense of responsibility.

Often the instant defense mechanisms come out, such as "I don't care" or more to the point "How does that affect me?" Besides the obvious answer that I give to those disappointing few ("If you do it again you will lose your job"), it is the concept of Self vs. The Company that we have not adapted. People my age do not see the company as their final resting place and therefore may not care about one upset customer, not completely understanding the possible implications. That one customer may have been an editor at a *newspaper, or one of the bigger accounts that the company is currently*

holding.

It is important to let the younger generations know that their

individual work affects the company and is appreciated. This does not mean

that you have to talk to them everyday but it does mean that they need to

understand that everyday makes a difference. A lot of kids now will see a job

as temporary, and are almost certainly not worried about losing it. They know

that there are other jobs out there and know that they can get them (yes, even

during a recession this thought pattern is prominent). This short sidedness can

be countered by appreciation. If someone is doing well, take a couple of

minutes to let them know. During that conversation let them know that you

have been following their performance for some time and you have noticed

improvements in the production. If that is not the case for an employee, pull

them aside and discuss. You will be astounded by the transparent and sometimes inappropriate answers you get. It could be a girlfriend at home, it could be a parent in the hospital and it could be as simple as "I just don't care anymore". All of them have answers and each answer depends on the relationship that has formed between you two. If you took time to stop and say hi, to ask for feedback, you will be able to truthfully say something like "Well I am sorry to hear that, we appreciate your work here and if there is anything I can do let me know, but I need you to focus on work right now." Simple and to the point.

Video games do not waste time letting us know that "our performance has been slightly decreasing and unfortunately is now to the point where it is a problem;" they say "FAILED." That is what we expect. That is what we are accustomed to and what we respond best to. No one likes losing or being told they are not able to complete a task, so let's address the issue and work on it, so it does not happen again.

The bottom line of what works is always offering an open avenue of communication. It focuses less on making a lot of goals and creating a long term vision, and more on paying attention to today and tomorrow. I do not want to think about six months from now, and frankly do not care; I may not even work here anymore. What I want to know is what is happening this week. Tell me how my day will be affected tomorrow if I do not complete A and B today. Tell me that my work is something that is recognized, and I may step it up to see if anyone really is watching. It is surprising how carefully we watch the reactions to our actions; we all test the waters to see how far we can push. The positive thing about that for a manager is that we also respect the boundaries when they are found and sternly addressed.

What's next?

"Planning is bringing the future into the present so that you can do something about it now." ~Alan Lakein

The first order of business is to make a plan. How can you make your company more successful while getting the most out of the workforce? What are some of the ways to keep employees motivated and feeling good about the work they do? Office rules are a good place to start. Always have core hours. Everyone has to be there between 9:00 am and 3:30 pm. Each employee can pick a start time but they must keep to it. Keep a casual dress code. There are some things you cannot allow, such as gang colors or vulgar language on shirts. It is just plain stupid for someone to wear a tee shirt with "Kill Bill" on it when your name is Bill.

Some ideas to entertain are: Close the office at 3:00 pm before a holiday weekend. Once an employee has 6 months of service the company will pay all of or part of their student loan. Pay tuition reimbursement on any subject. Any education is good education. Mandate 20 hours a year of volunteer activity.

Allow employees to use cell phones and stay up with their social networks during work hours. If an employee's performance suffers because they are on their cell phone all day, address the situation then. All other employees will be waiting for you to address an employee that abuses a privilege.

What's next depends on your situation. It depends on the work that is expected and how drastic of a change it will be. For example, if you require people to wear a suit and tie to work, then one day say the dress code is gone, it will be too drastic. People will perceive that as too big of a leap. If you require that people show up on time and then say that there is a 15 minute grace period, most of your younger employees will be showing up at 9:14.

Start small. Start by sending out an email saying that you want to meet personally with everyone for a 15 minute meeting for an update on the company's goals. Then talk to the employees and ask them questions. You can walk in with a blank sheet and leave each meeting with a full one. Ask them how they feel, ask how they like their job, and ask what you can do to make their day to day process easier. Have three bullet points on the person's performance. One good, one bad, and one that is neutral. Something like, "Last week you did great in sales and I wanted to take the time to let you know. What did you do that week that you did not do 2 weeks ago? That week was nowhere near as productive?" This is a good and a bad thing at the same time. You may even get an answer that has nothing to do with what you were thinking. Maybe they contacted their clients through Facebook™ instead of the phone and found it was easier to stay in touch. Maybe they have no idea. The point is you do not know until you ask. We will feel like our voices are not heard if you do not take the time to let us talk. Then address something neutral "I noticed that you clock in to work on time or close to it every day. Good job." It is something expected. It is something that should not have to be said. Yes, we are required to show up on time at any job, but taking the time to let us know you're keeping a close eye really contributes to the idea that I really matter at this company.

After you have a list of ideas from everyone, you can pick some of the feasible ones and decide what to do. If there are reoccurring themes in a lot of the discussions, you just found a trend. Find the reason multiple people are saying the same thing and address it. Maybe everyone the office says that the vending machine doesn't have anything good in it. FIX IT. Everyone says that they do not like their headsets. GET NEW ONES. If only a couple of people say one thing, then fix it for them. Let them know their voice was heard and something that is small is still important. Let the person sitting next to them who notices their new mouse and keyboard come to you and ask why they did not get one.

"I asked her what would make her job easier and she said her keyboard has sticky keys. I figured that's pretty important and get her a new one."

"Well I don't really like mine, it's too big"

"Ok no problem; I will see what I can do with that"

It is simple. They received because they asked. You knew because you asked them. This promotes the open channel of communication and demonstrates that management is open to suggestions. Any company that will not listen to an employee with a decent idea is doomed to be mediocre. I plan on greatness and expect the same of my employees. Part of that is teamwork and part of teamwork is compromise. If it is within my power to get a new keyboard or to get better food in the vending machine, you can guarantee I am going to do that.

I selected fairly simple issues for a couple of reasons. If a lot of people in the company cannot stand the receptionist, you can't fire him because he is annoying. I would not recommend doing anything even close to that! What you can do is pull him aside after the meetings and let him know where he needs to improve.

"I have gotten a lot of feedback that people are frustrated with how long it takes for you to answer the phone. How many times do you usually let it ring and can you pick up faster?"

"Well I am usually working on something else so I just like to finish up that real quick before I pick up."

"OK I can see where that makes sense, in the future if the phone rings that is first priority, ok?"

It is easy. Give someone a chance to defend their actions, let them know what needs to change and make sure they understand it. Telling us what to do and what not to do is expected. If we are never told what not to do, or if we do something wrong with no consequence, you can bet that you will see it occur much more frequently. We know you're in charge and expect it to happen.

When does it start?

"Nobody can go back and start a new beginning, but anyone can start today and make a new ending."` ~*Maria Robinson*

It starts with "Good morning," and stopping by an employee's workstation just to chat. Know what the company needs from each person. A job description is a good way to start. Human resources or the manager should write it. If you let the employee write their own job description it will be way too detailed and long. The employee-employer relation starts during the hiring process. What attracted the employee to the company? A good manager needs to get to know each person as individuals and as part of a team.

It starts with paying attention to minor and sometimes non work related details. If someone is in a band, then every once and a while ask how it is going. How are you going to remember that? TAKE NOTES. An employee file should no longer just be their legal information, disclosure agreement, benefit package and 401K. It needs to have a detailed personal section with some small talk that you can generate from. This lets them know you are listening and paying attention. I think most people my age expect our managers not to care about them. We expect them to ask questions in passing to pretend that they care, then instantly forget the answer. When you walk up to someone two weeks later and ask how their show went last Friday, you will have just gained the respect of an employee. Since we are not entirely focused on the company and its status, we are not going to always respond to banter about the work day.

Say something about the vacation I am planning or the sports team that

I talked about last Tuesday and you will see a friendly and receptive side of me you might have never met. Taking the time to go back to your office and write down that John likes motorcycles is something that will save you immeasurable time gaining trust. Like I said before, we do not need or really want to make new friends but have no problem switching to our friendly mode in a non-formal conversation.

Why will we be Successful?

"Successful and unsuccessful people do not vary greatly in their abilities. They vary in their desires to reach their potential." ~John Maxwell

Show each employee you care about the success of the company and the success of the individual. The obvious is to lead by example. Always be prepared and informed. If you are reading this paper you are looking for something. A secret to the success of the company is to stay curious and try new things. Not every idea will be a success. Some will be grand slams and some will be singles. A good manager needs to know how to learn from their failures.

We will be successful because we will take the time to learn how each employee feels and will follow up with small talk that is important to them. We will be successful because we took the time to understand what the differences are between us, address them and then move on to the next task. It is very easy to conceptualize changes and talk about them in meetings but the bottom line is this: The best answer is always to act.

Act on your instinct and blend it with the insight from this discussion. The concepts of caring about your employees and being direct when speaking to them is nothing new, it is just harder to do with people you can not relate too. Fortunately the fundamental principals of respect have not changed. You can not go wrong saying "good morning" to anyone and will not be seen as bizarre if you say "have a good night". The thing to remember is that you have taken the time to learn and sought guidance when unsure. Continuous education and keeping an open mind are monumental factors in being a *successful leader, keep them up and you will be fine. Managing the younger or the older generation requires a skill set of patience and understanding if you give your self and your employees the opportunities to work on them you will earn everyone's respect.*

Written by Patrick Joseph Corbet SPHR CLRP & Brian Patrick Corbet

Edited by Bridget Kathryn Corbet